Lyfe's

Chronicles

It Wasn't For Nothing

Tiwonna R. Moore

Dedication

This book is dedicated to my mother, Gloria Ann Bates, and my mother-in-law Mary Ann Moore.

Gone but never forgotten!

Acknowledgments

I would first like to acknowledge God the Father—this book would not be possible without His Grace and Mercy. I love Him and thank Him for sending His son Jesus Christ to die to save me. I thank the Father for giving me His precious Holy Spirit to lead, teach, and help me with those things that seem impossible to me. Father, thank you for the things that continue to cause me to dig deeper, finding treasures buried in this earth and vessels of clay for His Glory.

I thank and honor my husband, Jackson C. Moore, a priest, king, and prophet of our household. I can't imagine doing life without him. He pushes me to be better, brings out the best in me, and truly loves me as Christ loves the church.

I acknowledge my two children, Te'Yonna Moore and Jackson "Tyler" Moore, as the best children in the world. They have truly ministered to me through their short lives.

Sometimes, I wondered if I was raising them or if they were raising me. There were times when I was sick, and tiny hands would touch my head and pray to God for my healing. Other times they came together and prayed for our family, and God answered them.

I acknowledge my grandmother Willie Ruby Piper, who raised three generations. I knew I could count on my grandma no matter what I faced. She always told me, "If you need anything, let me know." At 90 years old, she still tells me the same thing.

I want to acknowledge my brother James Christopher Bates. When I truly needed him, he was always there. I know our mother would be proud of us.

I acknowledge my Pastor, Jackson G. Moore, my father-in-law. I thank him for being the man of God that he is. I thank him for not only accepting me as his daughter-in-law but his daughter. I thank him for raising Godly children that love and respect him.

I also thank my mother-in-law Leslie Moore for always being there for every birthday party and event that the kids have. She is a very present help.

I would also like to thank my church family (who is my family) and friends for their love and support throughout the years. I love you all and

pray for God's richest blessing upon your lives.
(You know who you are)

Lastly, I thank my many cousins who were my
childhood friends.

Table of Contents

"If what you do doesn't cause you to have total reliance on God's grace daily, then you have not yet reached the apex of your predestined calling."

Think bigger!

Tiwonna R. Moore

Introduction

"I have observed something else under the sun. The fastest runner doesn't always win the race, and the strongest warrior doesn't always win the battle. The wise sometimes go hungry, and the skillful are not necessarily wealthy. And those who are educated don't always lead successful lives. It is all decided by chance, by being in the right place at the right time. People can never predict when hard times might come. Like fish in a net or birds in a trap, people are caught by sudden tragedy." Ecclesiastes 9:11-12 (NLT)

Life is full of surprises and does not always look the same for everybody. According to King Solomon, predicting when challenging times will come is impossible. You can live an extraordinary life one day and then a life filled with trauma and adversity the next day. The uncertainties of life all stem from an adversary that many are not even aware exists. We are quick to blame others or become hard on ourselves when life tends to get hard without realizing we have an enemy seeking after us, like a roaring lion ready to kill, steal, and destroy our lives.

I know this to be a fact because my life has been filled with traumatic events meant to break me and keep me from fulfilling my God-ordained purpose. Over the course of my life, I have questioned the attacks and fiery darts that plagued my life. I, like many, often prayed, asking God, "Why me?" and wondering what I did to deserve such pain, agony, and rejection in my life. But no matter how much I questioned the roller coaster of life, it appeared I could never escape the ride until I learned to surrender all to God.

Life's Chronicles is a play-by-play of the struggles, hardships, dysfunction, and broken-ness I encountered from childhood to adult-hood. After years of seeking the Lord for healing and deliverance from the enemy's snares, the Holy Spirit impressed upon me to share my testimony to encourage others. It took me some time to arrive at a healthy place where I could finally stand on the Rock, which is Jesus Christ– the Chief Cornerstone.

Like Job, I adopted the mindset, "Though You slay me, yet will I trust you!" When I reached this point of faith in my journey, life drastically turned in the right direction, and I realized I wasn't thrown into the pit of darkness for nothing. God had a plan and a purpose written before I was knit in my mother's womb. I encourage you today to know that whatever has happened in your life, "It wasn't for nothing!"

God has a plan to get the glory from your life story. Yes, I know it has been complex and challenging. Yes, I know the pain that appears to keep rearing its ugly head at the wrong times. I know too well about sickness, death, abuse, neglect, rejection, church hurt, financial woes, etc. But I also know that God is a healer, and according to His word, He will not put more on you than you can bear, and most important of all, He is the Father of spirits (Hebrews 12:9).

We could be or do nothing outside the will of God because He is the Creator and Sustainer of all things. Does this mean He places each spirit in the body of His choosing for His purpose to be fulfilled on Earth? Yes! The Word of God says that He prepared Himself a body in the person of the man Jesus to redeem mankind back to Himself (Hebrews 10:5)

Could it be possible that God the Father prepared us a body and gave us the same charge that he gave Adam and Eve in the Garden in Genesis 1:28? God's first charge to Adam and Eve was to be fruitful and multiply. The warfare you have been experiencing has been to keep you from multiplying and experiencing abundant blessings! God didn't say to be seedful. He said, "Be fruitful." I believe the seed was already in us when he gave mankind this commandment.

How else can anything produce fruit without first having a seed? All we need to do is nurture what's already within us. This fruitfulness didn't only speak to having babies. There are a lot of people that have babies and aren't fruitful. Fruitfulness speaks to being a good steward of what God has blessed you with. Your children, however, can speak to your fruitfulness if they are stewarded well.

How well do we steward the gifts given by the almighty God? How do you govern or rule over the things that God has blessed us with? The world now differs from when Adam and Eve were here on Earth. So much has changed from Genesis 1:28 to Genesis 3:7. Could we, millions or billions of years later, carry out the same mandate God gave to the first man and women he created? If so, how can we carry this charge out in this sinful world? Will we be just like Adam and Eve and fail our assignment? I recall being a young girl in church, and we would sing the song "We Are Soldiers." The lyrics were very profound: *"We are soldiers in the army. We have to fight, although we have to cry. We have to hold up the bloodstained banner. We have to hold it up until we die!"*

I didn't understand the song at that time. I recall how excited and energized the church would get as people would stand on their feet and declare their position in the army of the Lord. We were ready for battle, or so we thought, because when the battle comes, many tend to go AWOL (absent without leave). We run from the battlefield and try to avoid the trenches.

But what is this battle about? Who is this fight against? Did we enlist in this army, or were we drafted in? I've only been on this earth for thirty-nine years, but many of these questions are becoming real. The Lord told me that I would go through a lot on this earth, but the trials I faced weren't about me but what God wants to do in and through me. The same thing applies to you, my sisters and brothers. We have been created to give God glory, which can only be achieved through trusting in Him and never leaning on our own understanding.

Take a journey with me through Life's Chronicles as we explore God's intentions and blueprint for our lives. I pray that my testimony will serve as a testament to your life to understand that nothing you have been through will be wasted and that *"It Wasn't For Nothing."*

Happy Reading! Tiwonna

Chapter One

"It's Just a Test"

Journaling has always been my favorite thing to do. I remember in middle school writing down something as simple as how I wore my hair and what I wore to school. Writing has always been an outlet for me, a way to express myself. I was always quiet, but I expressed myself through writing.

I started writing a little poetry in high school when I started having crushes in relationships and going through teenage breakups. I wrote about pain as I began to experience the heartaches of life, such as death, broken friendships, sickness, and fellowship with God.

Then at some point, I started writing about broken fellowship with God and challenging things that were sometimes too hard to journal. Revelation 12:11 (NLT) says, "And they have defeated him (Satan) by the blood of the Lamb (Jesus) and by their testimony."

Journaling allowed me to chronicle every facet of my life. At the time, I had no clue that I would write a book about my life to encourage others, but God did. Even though I didn't always understand my uniqueness, God created me to be exactly who He wanted me to be for His glory.

Romans 8:37-38 (NLT) says, "No, despite all these things, overwhelming victory is ours through Christ, who loved us. And I am convinced that nothing can ever separate us from God's love. Neither death nor life, neither angels nor demons, neither our fears for today nor our worries about tomorrow—not even the powers of hell can separate us from God's love." I love this scripture because it reassures me that no matter what happens in life, God is faithful to His promises and will perform His word. No matter what enemy rises against me, I have victory in Christ.

I remember watching TV in the late eighties, and in the middle of the program you were watching, there was a loud, annoying long beeeeeep. Following the long beep was the following announcement: *"This is a test of the Emergency Broadcast System. Broadcasters, in cooperation with the FCC and other authorities (or, in later years, "federal, state and local authorities"), have developed this system to keep you informed in the event of an emergency. Had this been an actual emergency, the attention Signal you just heard would have been followed by official information, news, or instructions."*

I cannot begin to tell you how annoying this beeping was, especially if the show was getting good because tv didn't have rewind and replay features like it does today. But after they were over in a few seconds, my show returned to the regularly scheduled program where it left off. The EBS of the eighties reminds me of life. You are in the middle of living your best life or transitioning from one phase in life to another when out of nowhere, an interruption takes place, and you become highly annoyed.

You don't know what to think. You find yourself trying to figure out what went wrong. How did things go left when they were going right? I don't know about you, but these were the questions I asked myself, only to find out these were my testing seasons. I wanted things to happen the same as the EBS–hear the sound, wait a few minutes, and then life will resume as normal. I mean, it was only a test, right? Not all the time! What if it wasn't a test but an actual emergency? 1 Peter 4:12 (KJV) instructs us to "Think it not strange concerning the fiery trial, which is to test you, as though some strange thing happened unto you."

Whether test or emergency, we are not supposed to be moved or think something strange is happening to us. We are expected to trust that if God brought us to it, He would get us through it.

Summer of 1987, I was twelve, and my brother was six. We were both living with my grandma at the time. We had the time of our lives, although we were not with our mom because she was in a drug rehab facility. A few months earlier, my grandma called in and had our mom picked up for drug use. My grandma's good friend lived in the row houses directly in front of our house where we lived with my mom. She told my grandma that my mom kept a lot of company and our lights were out.

I guess she knew the lights were out because she saw the extension cord being run from our house to the neighbor's house next door. Later I remember my grandma coming and picking us up to stay on what was supposed to be the weekend, and the next thing I knew, I was going to see my mom in a drug rehab facility. It wasn't so bad for me because I drank coffee and ate plenty of snacks when we visited her once a week. I remember my mom being distraught with my grandma and not even wanting to talk to her for the first couple of visits, but my mom eventually got over it.

Most of the summer was spent spending the nights with my two older cousins. I would be at their house, or we all would be at our grandma's house. Neither of them had siblings, so I was like their little sister. One summer evening, my cousins and I noticed that the adults seemed to be really down. My older cousin, who was four years older than me and two years older than the other, came to us with tears in her eyes and said, "I overheard them saying that somebody has cancer, and I think it's my mom."

Cancer was no stranger to our family. My great-grandfather had passed a few years earlier from colon cancer, and my grandma's sister not long after that from breast cancer. So, me and my cousin Nikky tried to comfort our cousin Shalunda while we wondered if it could be our mothers. But we wouldn't dare ask who had cancer, so we just waited for the news.

Almost a month went by, and we were beginning to think that Shalunda may have misheard the information about one of our moms having cancer, so we went about our summer having fun.

Chapter Two

"Mama, Don't Go!"

By now, the drug rehab was giving my mom day passes, and my grandma would pick her up and take her back in the evening. Well, on a one-day pass, my mom met up with her ex-boyfriend Victor, and when it was time to take my mom back to rehab, my mom wanted me and my brother to ride back with her, my grandma, and Victor. So, we piled up in the car. I rode in the front seat with my brother. My grandma was driving with my mom and Victor in the back seat.

I remember Victor and my mom looking mad at one another. My mom asked my grandma to turn the radio off, and then she said, "Tiwonna! Chris! I have something to tell y'all. I'm sick. I have AIDS." In the '80s, not much was known about AIDS. The only thing I remember is wondering if I could eat off the same plates and spoons without getting AIDS. I realized that Victor was sitting against the door as if he was going to contract the disease by touching her, but little did he know he had AIDS too.

Victor said to my mom, "I hope you didn't give it to me." My mom said, "For all I know, you could have given it to me! You just need to go get tested!" The silence on the way to the rehab was debilitating. Victor's whole body was pushed up to one side of the car in the back seat. My brother was playing with his toys. With tears in her eyes, my mother looked like she had been crying for days, and my grandmother fought back her tears. We pulled up to let my mother out at the drug rehab, and as we said our goodbyes, my brother looked up and said,

"Mom!"

"Yes, Chris."

"Do you still have AIDS?" "Yes, I do, son."

"Don't worry, Mom, you'll get better." He returned to playing with his toys.

My mom finally got out of rehab, and my brother and I went to live with her in some apartment complexes. My grandmother was there to help my mom get back on her feet, which appeared to be the norm. She bought me and my brother new bunk beds and furniture for the apartment because everything was lost when my mom went to rehab.

I started a new school, and despite the news of my mom's recent diagnosis, I was able to put everything at the back of my mind. The first day of school in the fifth grade was exciting. I was dressed from head to toe. I had on a pair of two-tone Converse tennis shoes to match my outfit. You couldn't tell me nothing!

I was sitting in my homeroom when the teacher began to call the roll, and she called a familiar name, Nelson Green. Nelson Green! I thought, bullied me at my previous school. However, no one answered after his name was called. Maybe it was another Nelson Green. All I could do was hope it wasn't my bully. Day two roll was called, but still no Nelson Green. Day three, guess who shows up? Yes, Nelson Green, the bully.

At lunch that day, Nelson had the nerve to sit by me. Since he didn't know anyone else, he sat down and began to talk to me like he had some sense. He asked me why I left the old school, and I told him we had moved. Everyone started to find out about my mom's diagnosis, so I went to live with my aunt and cousin. My aunt started dealing with drug problems, so I had to move back with my mom. In the earlier years of my life, I did a lot of moving around from family member to family member. I thank God I was not a part of the system because family members would step up even if they had their own personal struggles.

My mother was not married when I was born, and I never knew my biological father. When I was born, my mother was still in cosmetology school, and she could not care for me, so I went to live with my grandfather's aunt and her husband. They were old when I went to live with them at only a few months old. They didn't have children of their own, so they spoiled me.

When I was about six, my godmother had a stroke, and she could no longer care for me. My godfather worked full-time, and he and I were really close. He told me stories about him not being with me for long, but I never understood them. I vividly remember everything about them, even our house, because it was centered around me. The screened porch was filled with my toys.

When I was six, I returned to stay with my mom, who was pregnant with my brother. Not long after I left, my godmother passed away. I remember having a dream that was so real. In the dream, an angel came to get me from my bed and took me out the front door. As soon as I crossed out of my yard, I was at the front gate of my godfather's yard. He was seated on the porch, and I ran and hugged him and told him how much I missed him. He told me he would have to go away, but I didn't have to worry because he would always be with me.

I cried uncontrollably until the angel came to get me from his arms. As the angel took me away and crossed from his yard, we were back at my mom's house. I cried so hard that I was crying in my sleep and woke my mom up. When my mom asked me what was wrong, I was too emotional to tell her. About a week later, I found out that my godfather had passed away too.

When I started school, I was behind. I daydreamed a lot about being back with my godparents. The transition from living with my godparents to moving with my mom was challenging. I didn't know much about my mom. My grandmother and grandfather visited often, but I didn't remember seeing my mom. I held this against her for a long time. It felt like she had a tighter bond with my brother because she raised him.

Before my mom became really sick, I shared these feelings with my cousin, and she shared them with my mom. My mom then explained that she intended to return and get me after she finished school and got settled, but when she did, my godparents cried to keep me. They promised my mom that they would take good care of me.

She expressed how blessed I was to live with them because I had diamond earrings and things she could not provide as a single parent. So, she let me stay. She said it became more challenging for her to leave me each time she came to see me as a baby. So, she stopped coming as much. I somewhat understood, even though we were never close. I thank God for my godparents because they gave me a solid foundation. One that I hoped to build someday.

My mom was a good mother who never talked down on me and wanted better for me and my brother. Even though her surroundings overtook her, she had hope for our future. Sadly, that hope surrounded us, and we did not end up like her.

Due to the ignorance of AIDS and the widespread fear, we were told to tell everyone that my mom had cancer. The thought of losing her to this disease never crossed my mind. I always envisioned my mom as a superwoman, like most kids. It didn't hit me that she could lose her life to this disease until our next-door neighbor died. She was my mother's age and had two kids our age. My mom had me go to the funeral with her. Everybody knew that she had died from AIDS because of the small neighborhood we grew up in.

I remember someone telling my mom how AIDS had affected her brain and how before she died, she went blind. Hearing those rumors gave my mom little to no hope. Because no one knew that my mom, too, had AIDS, they loaded her down with bad report after bad report about the physical challenges of the next-door neighbor before she passed away.

The night we went to the funeral, I remember it being a lot of cars and having to park on the street and walk far. My mom looked at me and said, "Do you know this will soon be me?" I just looked blankly, refusing to believe what she was saying, and as she began to cry, I didn't know what to say. I just believed she was different and would somehow beat this disease.

As my mom grew weak and frail, we moved in with my grandmother and grandfather. My cousin Nikky was already living with my grandma. After school, we focused on caring for my mom. Sometimes I would get picked up from school and taken to the hospital to sit with her in the ER. It seemed that my grandma was unable to care for my mom. After being with her all day, she needed a break in the evening when we came home from school. My cousin Nikky helped us care for my mom, but I remember sitting in the ER many times by myself with my mom.

One weekend we went to Nikky's mom's house in the country to get a break, and that trip was cut short because my mom fell asleep, and no one could wake her up. I was taken from my aunt's house in the country to the hospital to sit with my mom in the ER. When the doctor entered the room, my mom asked how much time he thought she had left. He said about two weeks and walked out. Well, she was dead in a week. Proverbs 18:14 says, "A person's spirit can endure sickness, but who can survive a broken spirit?"

People are healed from debilitating illnesses every day. But it is the inner willingness of that individual that will determine if they overcome the disease or the disease defeats them. My mother's soul was broken before the disease ever attacked her body. Therefore, she had lost before she even began to fight. My mom lost her life to AIDS at the young age of 36 years old. And this was not the only health challenge she had in her life because she smoked cigarettes, which caused her lung problems. I remember my brother begging her to stop because no child wants to lose a parent.

During this phase of my life, I did not understand that I was in the classroom of life. I did not know that there would be chapters of my life that included various lessons to test my ability to navigate to the next place. Today I understand these things had to happen. No matter how hard or unfair it may have seemed, God had a plan that wasn't based on my thoughts because He planned my life before I was conceived. He knew I would be a motherless child at fifteen.

I had so many people telling me I don't know how you did what you did. From age twelve until two weeks before my fifteenth birthday, I helped take care of my mother to the point I had to change her pamper, help her bathe, and put on clothes. I don't remember nurses or family members coming over to help other than my cousin, who is a year and a half older than me.

The only answer I can give is that sometimes you have to do what you have to do. Sometimes, people make decisions that affect not only them but everyone close to them. Yet even in that, God promises to work EVERYTHING for the good of those who love him and are called according to his purpose for their lives (Romans 8:28)."

At the time, no one could convince me that losing my mom could ever work for my good. It wasn't God's will for my mom to die. She made a choice that did not produce a harvest of abundant life but led to an early grave. The wage of sin is death, and God's gift is eternal life. God is sovereign and has given each person the grace to choose life or death, blessings or curses.

He knows the decisions we will make and how those decisions will affect us and those we love. Knowing our choices and that we have free will allows each situation to work out in our favor IF we love and trust God. We can sit and think about all the what-ifs, which will do us no good. God, the Father, has already factored in the what ifs for us and has given us the best possible outcome for us to be who he has called us to be.

James 1:2-4 (AMP) says, *"Consider it nothing but joy, my brothers and sisters, whenever you fall into various trials. Be assured that the testing of your faith [through experience] produces endurance [leading to spiritual maturity and inner peace]. And let endurance have its perfect result and do thorough work, so that you may be perfect and completely developed [in your faith], lacking in nothing."*

Just like that long, annoying beep that interrupted television shows of the '80s, this tragedy interrupted the prime of my teenage life. However tragic this event was, it was only a test. Even though I was young, I had some experiences with God, but now I had to take my dependence on Him to another level. *"Even if my father and mother abandon me, the Lord will hold me close."* Psalms 27:10 (NLT)

Chapter Three

"God Did It!"

1996 Journal Entry

"EVERYTHING GOD HAS DONE FOR ME"

No way home from school. God made a way. My friends didn't understand their problems. God gave me something to say. I didn't know what I was going to do about money for prom. God made a way. Things I used to do; God took that away. The way I used to talk; God gave me something better to say. Things I used to do; God took it all away.

Hate I'd used to feel God took it away. Places I used to go; God led me in a different way. Just this morning, God made a way. He woke me up to see another day. Problems I have, I give them to him, Jesus died on the cross, and I don't have to worry about them.

Tiwonna Bates 1996

I pinned this journal entry when I was nineteen years old. I had moved from living with my grandma, grandpa, and little brother to living with my aunt and her new husband. My grandma's old fashion ways drove me crazy, and I was counting down until high school graduation, even though I had no plans of where I would live after graduation.

My aunt was newly divorced and came to live with my grandparents. My aunt saw how miserable I was and promised to take me with her as soon as she found a job and somewhere to live. She found that job, a place to live, and a new husband, which meant I couldn't just up and leave as anticipated.

Well, one day, my grandma took me to a level of no return, and I was not about to stay in that house another day. I called my aunt, and her response was like music to my ears. She told me I could move in with her and her husband. Hallelujah! Thank you, Jesus!

So, I did, and everything was good. When I moved in with my aunt, I agreed to give her fifty dollars a month because I only received two hundred and fifty dollars from my mom's social security each month.

I was free to come and go without being asked questions or having to justify how long I stayed out. Life was going well until they informed me, they were moving to take a job driving eighteen-wheelers. I thank God my aunt and her husband did not find a job assignment until after graduation. I would have been stuck without anywhere to go. But God! After I graduated, I found a summer job, plus I did my aunt's hair every couple of weeks. I guess you can say it was compensation for living with her.

Here I was again, going through another phase of life, trying to figure things out while learning lessons that were challenging, yet preparing me for my future. I was back at square one, not knowing where I would live. The school of my dreams was right around the corner from my aunts' house. When other kids talked about being doctors and going to space, I wanted to do hair. My mother was known as one of the best hair stylists in Fifth Ward, Texas.

I was a visual learner and would sit and watch her transform women's lives daily. She mostly did all types of hair in the kitchen and was a great enthusiast. She worked those Marcel curling irons and scissors while smoking her Kool Filter Kings cigarettes. I knew how to do a little hair because I watched my mom, plus my grandma was a hairdresser who styled Tina Turner and cut Bobby Blue Bland's hair. Doing hair is in my blood.

After my mother began getting sick, I started cutting and curling a few of her client's hair when I was only thirteen. When I was in the eleventh grade, I decided to go to cosmetology school but was unsure which one to attend.

One weekend on our way to Montgomery, Texas, a radio commercial advertised the San Jacinto College Cosmetology program. As I looked to my right, we passed the San Jacinto River, and I thought this was a sign.

I took down the number and called and received a packet by mail. I couldn't believe the school had a 99 percent pass rate for the state board. I had to go there! With my aunt and her husband moving, what was I to do? I started school at San Jacinto College North Campus in August 1996 and was finally living my dream. But that dream did not come without struggle. I had to make some sacrifices.

I ended up living with my friend Brenda, who lived with her foster mom Faye. She told me I could live with them for free if I went to school or worked. Faye had two daughters and three other foster girls. She was really cool. She let us go out and have fun as long as we took care of business, which meant everyone had their share of house cleaning to do. We would give her a hard time here and there. She would tell us to clean up, and she would leave, and when she came back, we would all be gone. She would fuss and cuss, and we would all laugh about it later.

Living with my friend was very humbling, to say the least. I thought I had it bad because all my cousins had a mom and dad, and my mom passed away and didn't have a dad either. I often wondered why me. The night I left my aunt, I felt abandoned. My grandma said I could come back, but my grandpa didn't want to have kids and teens around. The social security I received from my mom's passing was long gone because I had graduated from high school.

Due to my mom's drug usage, we moved every few years, but I knew I could always live with my grandma for stability. So now I felt like I was living with strangers. I had known Brenda for less than a year. My grandma would check on me and take me here and there to get things for school. But even my uncle, who adopted me, grew tired of paying for my schooling. I was learning to navigate life alone at a young age because I lacked family support.

As long as I could be filed as a dependent on taxes, welfare, and social security, it was all good, but when the perks ran out, the support ran out. I felt rejected, and this was not a good feeling. The spirit of rejection can destroy a person's life because that individual is willing to do anything or be with anyone to feel relevant and wanted.

I can't say this was the case with all my family members, but I don't remember anyone reaching out to check on me other than my grandma. Even in my sinfulness, I knew that God had my back. It was indeed His goodness that led me to repentance. I couldn't hold on to the bitterness I so desperately thought I deserved to have.

God always showed Himself faithful in every situation. Sometimes God will allow man's rejection to accrue to draw you to Him. He wants you to know that He is a friend who sticks closer than a brother (Proverbs 18:24). God showed me that even when my mother and father forsake me, He will receive me (Psalms 27:10). I had unforgiveness toward my mother too. I wondered why she couldn't do better or be better if not for herself, for me, and for my brother.

And you saw how the Lord your God cared for you all along the way as you traveled through the wilderness, just as a father cares for his child. Now he has brought you to this place. Deuteronomy 1:31 (NLT)

You keep track of all my sorrows. You have collected all my tears in your bottle. You have recorded each one in your book. Psalm 56:8 (NLT)

Now I know that there was a purpose in my pain. With God, nothing is ever wasted. He even stores up our tears. Life is a teacher, and even though I was angry with her, I realized I was in no position to judge because I was not perfect. I did things knowing that it could have cost me my life. But God kept me in my foolishness. I always heard the seasoned saints say we would understand it better by and by.

Living with Brenda allowed me to see that even though I lost my mom, she didn't neglect, abuse, or abandon my brother or me. Some of the girl's parents were accused of sexual abuse, and my friend's biological mom gave her up for a man. Brenda and I shared a small room. She had a full-size bed. I slept at one end, and she slept at the other end. After a few months, we weren't as close as I thought, and we were not getting along anymore. I started sleeping on the couch in the living room. Because of the abandonment that Brenda experienced, it was hard for her to trust, so there was some pent- up anger, and these underlying emotions in our lives ended our friendship. After about eight months, I found myself moving again.

My brother had more stability because he lived with my grandmother most of the time, even when my mother was alive. We were six years apart in age, so we weren't very close. He was more like the annoying little brother that asked my boyfriends for a dollar if they wanted to talk to me without him being in our faces. Not to mention that he was a tattle tell even when I gave him money not to. When we both lived with my mom, we were closer. We would listen to music together, and I would make up dance moves for us to do together.

I missed the life I had before losing my mom. It wasn't perfect, but at least we were together. If my mom were alive, I wouldn't have to go from pillar to post looking for a place to lay my head. My friend Lakycia from elementary got her own apartment, and I ended up over there most of the summer. I was able to finish two semesters of school. At that point, I started to get calls saying that Faye wanted me to pick up my things, which were only a few clothes and shoes, a TV, VCR, and a "Waiting to Exhale" VHS. After moving out of my grandma's house, my belongings got less and less. I started with a full-size bedroom set, radio system, 32-inch TV, clothes, and shoes and ended up with little to nothing.

Brenda and I would joke about how we started with a lot but ended up like the cartoon characters with the stick and handkerchief hanging from the end. When I picked up my things from Faye's house, all the girls acted cold toward me. Faye asked me what was going on. I told her that I was told that she wanted me to come and get my things. She told me that she never told them that and didn't care what any of them said about me being there. She said I had a place to stay as long as I worked or went to school. I thanked her but knew it was time for me to move on.

While living with my friend Lakycia, I worked a summer job, but being friends or even best friends is different from being roommates. After staying with Lakycia, having fun, and partying most of the summer, it was time to return to the real world. My cousin Shon had gotten her own apartment and was a dental assistant. I moved once again from Northeast Houston to southwest Houston with my cousin. I re-enrolled back in school, but now I was about thirty-five miles away from the school of my dreams. I could have gone to a closer school, but I wanted to go to the best of the best. I stayed in school for one semester and lived off financial aid, but it wasn't enough.

Journal Entry 9/11/1997

On Thursday, God made a lot of things possible. First of all, he woke me up to see this day. Secondly, I was granted financial aid. Now I know what God means when he says, "Ask, and you shall receive, seek and you shall find, knock and the door shall be open."

Now I know that no matter what happens in my life, it is for a reason, and no matter what, God will be with me until the end.

God is good because I almost gave up on cosmetology school because of money. When I was in high school, my uncle adopted me so my brother and I could have medical insurance. I knew he made a lot of money, and this could affect my getting grant money. So, I told my uncle about my plans to go to school and showed him a brochure with the cost breakdown. After giving my uncle the brochure, he said don't worry about it; he would take care of it.

My uncle has a well-known oil and gas company job, so I didn't think $2,500.00 would break the bank, but I heard my grandma complaining every year about him claiming us on his taxes and never giving her anything. My uncle gave my grandma his credit card the first semester to get all my supplies and pay my tuition.

When the next semester came around, I received a phone call from my uncle telling me about his great idea. The "GREAT IDEA" was that I could apply for a student loan, pay my tuition, and pay him back the $1529.19 he had already spent on my schooling. (Down to the change).

I simply said, "Okay, I'll check into it." I was devastated. I went to the counselor's office in tears. He told me not to worry and that we would work something out so I wouldn't have to drop out of school. He asked me one simple question. "Who have you lived with the last two years"? I said, "my grandma." My uncle adopted me on paper, and I never lived with him one day. The college counselor told me to bring all my grandma's social security paperwork for her income. Not only did I qualify for a loan, but I also qualified for a grant.

In the process, I also applied for a scholarship from the cosmetology department, and I received that too! God is so awesome! This situation taught me never to give up. God will close one door so that He can open a bigger one. Now that God had worked that out, I realized moving in with my cousin Shon was a big challenge. Shon lived about thirty miles from my school. Oh, and I did not have a car. There was another school half the distance, but that school was not the best of the best.

In 1996 San Jacinto College had a 99 percent pass rate for the State Board. So, I made the sacrifice. The second week I had to take a trash bag the size of materials (around sixteen gallons) to school. I knew this would be impossible on the bus. Not to mention the one-plus miles I had to walk, so I reached out to my grandma. She was helping my cousin take care of her kids, and these were her great-grandchildren. She said she couldn't take me because she had to take them to school.

She told me to try my uncle, who lived on this side of town. I called my uncle, but he had to go to work. I was hopeless, and in tears, I vowed that the next time I would see my grandmother was at her funeral. I sat in the bathroom and cried my heart out. Here I am after the tragic loss of my mother, now having to tackle life with no family support. At least I was trying to make a life and career for myself.

What was I to do now? Hair was the only thing I knew. The Holy Spirit quickened me about the vow I had made against my grandma.

The Lord said, "If you make this vow, you will go no further than you are now, REPENT!"

With tears still in my eyes and a heavy heart, I asked God to forgive me. As soon as I asked the Lord for forgiveness and His help in this situation, my cousin Shon knocked on the door and said, "I know one other person that may be able to give you a ride." She was our other cousin on Shon's side of the family.

I had no other options, so I said to give her a call. When she called Keri, not only could Keri give me a ride the following day she actually went to the same school I attended! I couldn't believe it. I was like, "Let me talk to her. I asked her why she was going to school so far from where she lived." Her answer was the same as mine. She said, "Because it was the best school for her field of study." She was going to school to be an LVN and had to be at school simultaneously as I did.

The only problem was that she got out of school two hours earlier, but it didn't matter. God still gave me favor so that my classmates would give me a ride to the bus stop. God is so faithful. The moment I let go of the hurt with tears still in my eyes, God opened a better door. Not only did I have a ride to school for one day, but I also had a ride to school for the whole semester. God wants to do over and above all that we can think or imagine.

I would have never imagined someone else making the same sacrifice I made to be the best in their field of study. God is a perfector of all things, and He knows how to shift the impossible into possible. I am grateful for the destiny helpers God has placed in my life over the years.

Chapter Four

"A Spiritual Transition"

The hand of God was heavy upon my life while I was in school. He gave me favor with Him and man. He opened up doors, and believe it or not, I didn't do anything to deserve it. I knew of God, but I wasn't living for Him. It was His goodness that led me to know Him. After finishing that semester, I finally had to get a job to get my own place.

At that time, Brenda and I reconnected. She graduated from high school and got a job at the Galleria mall as a security guard. She told me they were hiring, so I applied and got the job. Most of my time after school was spent traveling on the bus. I became a shampoo tech for a lady who owned a salon, but that wasn't enough to supply my needs. After getting the security job Shon and I agreed it was time for me to move. Three months after I got the job, I got my own apartment. Praise God! We can often look at our lives and even feel sorry for ourselves but trust me; it's always someone that has it worse off than you.

I found a one-bedroom apartment for a little over three hundred dollars a month. I needed furniture, so I saved up and bought a few things before getting a department store credit card to finish fixing my little apartment. I even saved up to get a little run- down cash car for $1,200.00.

I moved into my apartment with only a bed, mattress, a small TV, VCR, and that "Waiting to Exhale" VHS, but I was happier than I had been in a long time. I remember rolling around from one side of the floor to the other, but it was mine. For the first time in a long time, I felt at home, and most importantly, it was mine.

It appeared as if my life was finally coming together. I worked and partied and partied and worked until New Year's Eve of 1997. I was excited about the New Year and ready to get my party on when I almost lost my life. I went out to a nightclub. They announced they were doing a money-release balloon drop. Well, who doesn't want free money? I do! Plus, I needed a little extra cash with all the new responsibilities.

I got into a battle-ready mode for the balloon release and was stepped on and almost knocked over. After leaving with a busted toe, lost eyeglasses, and no money from the balloon drop, I knew I was done with clubbing. Man, 1999 snuck up on me because all I did in 1998 was work overtime. I kept thinking I would be alright if I could only get a job. Then I thought I would be okay if I could only get my own apartment. Then I thought I would be alright if I could only get a car. But none of these things gave me the peace of mind I needed the most.

I had a friend from elementary school who partied harder than me, skipped school, and smoked weed, "the whole nine" (as we used to say), but she had accepted Christ into her life and was a completely different person. She appeared to have the joy and peace I was searching for. My friend invited me to church, but I was always working.

Then she told me about a new church her stepmom and dad went to where this woman pastor was off the chain. She was known for speaking the truth in a way that could be easily understood. So, after much convincing without letting up, I told myself, let me go and see what's so special about this pastor. I witnessed the fruit in my friend's life, and I thought if God could change her; I know there was help for me.

Journal Entry 01/05/1999

On January 3rd, 1999, I accepted the Lord into my life. I thank the Lord for the many things He has blessed me with, but what good would it be to gain the whole world and lose your soul? I know that nothing good is going to come out of gaining the world if I don't have the Lord Jesus Christ (1 John 2:15 NLT). Do not love this world nor the things it offers you, for when you love the world, you do not have the love of the Father in you.) So now it's 1999, and it's only been three days since I've given my life back to the Lord, and I still feel weak in some areas, but yet and still I know the Lord will bless and strengthen me in his word so that in the end I will be with him.

The first time I went to church, it was a part of my New Year's resolution of needing to get my life together. I never intended to join this church, but I did! The pastor spoke regarding every area of my life I was in at the time. She was all in my business. I knew deep down that my goal of returning to cosmetology school would not bring true happiness. I needed this. I needed to be in a place where I could hear God speak to me through His vessel, and I needed to be in a good place to hear Him for myself.

Journal Entry 01/31/1999

Today is the day that the Lord has made, and I will rejoice and be glad in it. I thank the Lord for the strength to stay in his well. I am making a vow to the Lord, and I won't go back. There is nothing good and no purpose for living for the devil.

Roman 6:21 says, "What benefit did you reap at that time from the things you are now ashamed of? Those things result in death!"

Journal Entry 04/05/1999

Salvation is the easy part, but sanctification is not so easy. My flesh still wanted to do the same old things. I met someone I worked with and set boundaries at first, but I let my guard down after some time.

Sanctification means a person is set apart for God's use, purpose, and plan. Sanctification is a continuous process that we will go through as long as we are in this body of flesh.

I take comfort in Romans 7:7-25 (ESV).

The Law and Sin

What, then, shall we say? That the law is sin? By no means! Yet, if it had not been for the law, I would not have known sin. For I would not have known what it is to covet if the law had not said, "You shall not covet." But sin, seizing an opportunity through the commandment, produced in me all kinds of covetousness. For apart from the law, sin lies dead. I was once alive apart from the law, but when the commandment came, sin came alive, and I died. The very commandment that promised life proved to be death to me. For sin, seizing an opportunity through the commandment deceived me and, through it, killed me. So, the law is holy, and the commandment is holy and righteous and good. Did that which is good, then, bring death to me? By no means! It was sin, producing death in me through what is good, in order that sin might be shown to be sin, and through the commandment might become sinful beyond measure. For we know that the law is spiritual, but I am of the flesh, sold under sin. For I do not understand my own actions. For I do not do what I want, but I do the very thing I hate. Now if I do what I do not want, I agree with the law, that it is good. So now it is no longer I who do it, but sin that dwells within me. For I know that nothing good dwells in me, that is, in my flesh. For I have the desire to do what is right but not the ability to carry it out. For I do not do the good I want, but the evil I do not want is what I keep on doing. Now if I do what I do not want, it is no longer I who do it, but sin that dwells within me. So, I find it to be a law that when I want to do right, evil lies close at hand. For I delight in the law of God, in my inner being, but I see in my members another law waging war against the law of my mind and making me captive to the law of sin that dwells in my members. Wretched man that I am! Who will deliver me from this body of death? Thanks be to God through Jesus Christ our Lord! So then, I myself serve the law of God with my mind, but with my flesh, I serve the law of sin.

I wanted to do what was right. My mind was made up to do what was right, but I didn't understand spiritual laws. In my mind, I served God, but the flesh will never be renewed. Sin was driving me away from God, but thank God for Jesus! Jesus is the LIVING WORD... When we decide to operate in the spirit by making the word of God higher than anything else, we find victory over the flesh.

There are three Laws at work:

1. The law of the spirit (law of God)
2. The law of sin (the law of the flesh)
3. The law of the mind (soul)

God's word tells us, "You shall love the Lord your God with all your heart, soul, and mind." Matthew 22:37 (ESV) However, we can't serve God out of an unrenewed mind. An unrenewed mind is dominated by Satan and his demons or by our flesh. The law of my members (flesh) was waging war against the law of my mind and making me captive to the law of sin that works in my flesh (members).

I serve God with my mind (renewed mind, not fleshly mind). I serve God by allowing His word to wash my mind so that the carnal mind (ruled by the flesh) is being washed with God's word and the spiritual man (a mind ruled by the Holy Spirit) can stand against the dictates of the flesh. We don't fight flesh with spirit. We fight Spirit to spirit.

"For though we walk in the flesh, we are not waging war according to the flesh. For the weapons of our warfare are not of the flesh but have divine power to destroy strongholds. We destroy arguments and every lofty opinion

raised against the knowledge of God, and take every thought captive to obey Christ, being ready to punish every disobedience, when your obedience is complete." 2 Corinthians 10:3-6

We have been losing the battle because we are fighting flesh to spirit, not Spirit to spirit.

"But God, being rich in mercy, because of the great love with which he loved us, even when we were dead in our trespasses, made us alive together with Christ—by grace, you have been saved— and raised us up with him (Jesus) and seated us with him in the heavenly places in Christ Jesus, so that in the coming ages he might show the immeasurable riches of his grace in kindness toward us in Christ Jesus." Ephesians 2:4-7 (ESV)

Jesus said that we are far above ALL PRINCIPALITIES. We must ascend to a level that is higher than the enemy to win.

Chapter Five

"God or Man?"

Compromise is a word that we tend to take lightly because many individuals like myself believe in giving the benefit of the doubt. The reason to doubt could be staring us right in the face, but we will ignore it and eventually find out the hard way that our first instinct should have been the one we listened to. But the classic cliché says, "A hard head makes a soft behind!" because if you keep falling for the okie doke, eventually you will get the overall picture and not desire to feel the pain anymore.

In the last chapter, I bragged about my new life in Christ and how good God is. And don't get me wrong, that did not change, but when I decided to change, I was presented with a very handsome distraction. I was determined to make God my choice and did just that when I kicked my new boo to the curve, but the enemy doesn't fight fair.

Journal Entry 04/21/1999

God, through his son Jesus Christ, died for me and all my past, present, and future sins. It's been God who will never leave my side nor forsake me. So, therefore, I decided to make Jesus my choice. I gave up that past relationship. When you are in a relationship and compromise your beliefs for someone else or for your own sinful desires, you are headed toward a dead end.

I wanted to do things the right way, but a relationship is a two-way street. I had to make a choice, and I chose to turn away from that relationship. After breaking that relationship off, I decided to focus on church and work. Lord knows that this mind needs to be renewed, but a lot can happen in a month.

Now, I did what I was supposed to according to the word of God. I put off my flesh to walk in the spirit, not after the flesh. I stayed focused for a good thirty-something days, but then my flesh kicked in, renewing my mind took a back seat, and I shifted my focus from living for Christ and being holy to being in a whole relationship.

This is when "compromise" knocked on my door, and I didn't peep through the peephole; I opened the door, and standing on the other side was an opportunity.

Journal Entry 05/31/1999

First of all, I would like to thank God for another day. It's been a month and ten days since I wrote last. Since last month a lot of things have happened. First of all, I am dating someone else; secondly, he has moved in with me.

Things are moving fast, but nothing has ever felt so right to me than what we have, and even though by God's command, I am living in sin, I truly feel that he will one day be my husband. We have so much in common, and we think a lot alike. We have the same beliefs about what a relationship should be. We also have the same beliefs in God.

I just knew that with all my heart that this new guy was the one for me. Despite going against God's word, I felt like I could make things right one day by simply getting married. That's what we all think, right?

Marriage makes everything right–right?

Did you read that entry? Looking back on it now, I can't believe I was trying to manipulate God to gratify my flesh. I knew right from wrong, but I also knew what I wanted, and Jackson seemed to have most of those qualities. One day I was at work, and I could not stop thinking about him and how special he made me feel. He brought me so much joy and happiness that it felt like a fairy tale, so much so that I allowed him to move in with me after he moved out with his ex-girlfriend.

I had just broken up with my boyfriend not even thirty days prior. However, Jackson and I had a history, so he wasn't a complete stranger. I started working a security job in December 1997 after I had finished my second semester in cosmetology school. I was staying with my cousin Shon with no money. My friend Brenda, whom I lived with before, started a job working security in the Galleria mall, and she told me about the security job. I applied for the job and was hired.

I had to attend a two-week training, and in my class was none other than Jackson Moore, A.K.A Officer Moore. I didn't have a car then, so I rode the bus, and Jackson would get on the bus at one of the stops. My first impression of Jackson was that he was weird. He wore a long black trench coat even though it was not cold. I would think that one day somebody will make him mad, and he will pull a shotgun from under that jacket. It's funny but true.

After the training, I worked the day shift, and he worked the night shift, so I didn't see him on the bus anymore. One morning I came into work and heard that the Galleria three area had been broken into, and one of the night shift guys had run the thief down and detained him. This may sound heroic, but as security officers, we were not allowed to make arrests.

Our job was to observe and report. If we saw a crime, we kept an eye on the criminal and reported it to the base, and the base would report it to HPD. However, the night officer, Officer Jackson Moore, wrestled the person down and held him. Oh, and by the way, he didn't have handcuffs because we were not allowed to make an arrest.

So, because of this, he was transferred to Transco Tower, which was right across the street. Everybody talked about what happened, but for the life of me, I couldn't remember who Jackson was. Some people told me he was in our training class, but it took me a while to figure out who he was. I think someone said the guy who always wears the black trench coat, then I remembered.

After a couple of years, I started working overtime security at other locations. One of those locations were Transco Tower. However, when I began working overtime, he was no longer there. One day the Sergeant said to me, "Officer Bates, you might lose your overtime because Officer Moore is coming back." I was like, "Who is Officer Moore"? He said, "You don't remember him?" I said, "No," he said you'll remember him when he gets here next week. He used to work at the Galleria night shift before coming over here.

His name still didn't ring a bell until I was working the night shift, and he came walking in. When I saw him, I thought, "Oh, the weird guy that used to wear the trench coat." He wasn't very friendly at first. He worked from 11 pm to 7 am, and I came in from 10 pm until 3 am. After leaving my 2 pm to 10 pm second shift, I would head straight to Transco Tower. I worked hard and was dedicated to my work, but little did I know God had something in the works that I would have never imagined.

Chapter Six

"How Did You Get Here?"

There is a classic cliché that says, "Nothing change, nothing changes!" I was working my butt off, but was I making changes. Was I making any life progress based on how it started and the hardships I endured over the years? I was determined to make my life count for something. At a young age, I had already lost so much, and I owed it to myself not to lose anything that was within my control.

After getting a vehicle I transferred my security assignment downtown to one of the office buildings. When I worked with the male security guards, they let me sit at the desk while they walked around. But I can't say the same about Officer Moore. When I got to work, and he was at the desk, he sat there and did not move. He didn't talk much, either. I would get my keys from him and turn them into him at the end of my shift. One night after turning in my keys, he said, "What's wrong with you women?"

With a shocked look, I asked, "Are you talking to me?" Then he said, "There is no one else in this big lobby but us, so who else would I be talking to?"

I said, "I didn't think you could talk because you never said anything. One question turned into a two-hour conversation. We both learned we were dealing with similar relationship issues. We felt like we gave more than we received and were fed up. We both worked very hard, and our significant did not. It seemed we wanted the same things out of life, but there was only one problem, he lived with his girlfriend, and I didn't want to come in between his relationship.

Weeks passed, and I continued working overtime with him. I think we talked more than we worked. I even came to his job just to talk to him when I was off. We were spending a lot of time getting to know one another, so I told him again that I was not trying to come in between him and his girlfriend. I suggested backing off until he figured out what he wanted to do. At this point, it was evident that he liked me just as much as I liked him. How did we get here?! Office Moore seemed cold and disconnected, but he was friendly, intelligent, hardworking, and, most of all, someone who wanted many of the same things I wanted. We had so much in common.

A few days later, I received a phone call from Jackson saying that he and his girlfriend got into a big argument, and he was ready to leave. This sounded good to me because now we could develop a relationship, but the next thing he asked shocked me. He asked me if he could stay at my place for a couple of weeks until he found his own place. I was feeling him, but not enough to let him move in because this would require a different type of commitment.

I asked him about the possibility of living with his mom and dad. But he felt like a grown man should never return home to his parents. I could understand that, but this was going to be interesting. I told him I would think about it because I liked him, but we hadn't known each other long enough to move in together.

My whole life, I felt like I never had a stable place to live. We were constantly bouncing around. After leaving my godparents, I moved in with my mom, and from my mom, I stayed with my grandma, and from my grandma, I lived with my aunt and cousins in different households.

After my mom died, I was supposed to move in with one of my aunts, but I stayed with my grandma because I felt she was unstable. I did not need any more instability in my life. As a child, I may not have known what a stable environment was, but subconsciously I longed for one.

Most children crave stability, whether they realize it or not. I just wanted a stable home life that didn't consist of feeling like I was being tossed and driven all the time. Whenever I thought I was settled, it was time to move again. I went from my grandma to another aunt, to a foster home, to my elementary friend roommate situation, and then to another cousin before getting my own place.

At first, I was scared of living in my own apartment, and watching tv didn't help. I watched those shows about someone breaking in, killing, and raping helpless women. Can you say the spirit of fear kicked the door in and made itself at home? Eventually, I stopped watching those shows and started going to church. Then and only then was I delivered from the spirit of fear and able to feel comfortable living alone.

So, I'm finally okay with being alone, and now someone wants to invade my space. I had to think long and hard about this decision. He only asked to stay for two weeks. I mean, what could happen in fourteen days? He wasn't a complete stranger because I knew where he worked. Jackson seemed to be stable because we had been working together for almost two years, other than the time he worked offshore. He had a good reputation and was able to come back because of his mother being sick.

When I weighed the pros against the cons, the pros won, and I called him and told him he could move in. I was nervous, but it was too late to turn back now. Jackson moved in with me on May 20th, 1999. He got off work that morning and headed straight to my apartment. He knocked on the door, and when I opened it, he began bringing his things in. I said, "Make yourself at home!" I could not believe I was sharing my humble abode with another man.

Deborah Cox sings a song, "How Did You Get Here?" As the days passed, I asked myself this question because I ended a relationship to ensure it did not interfere with my relationship with God, and here I was again, digging an even deeper hole.

Chapter Seven

"When The Storm Comes"

Journal Entry 6/6/99

"A LETTER TO GOD"

Dear God,

Today is a beautiful Sunday. It's now 1:49 pm. I just got out of church service and feel convicted in some areas of my life. My desire is to do your will and for your love and grace to rain on me. Lately, I haven't felt your presence because I have been shutting you out.

For the past month or two, I have let the devil get to me in some areas where I am weak. I have not been going to church as I should, but I still refuse to give the devil the victory. Today I went to church, and I realized many things. First, I'm living in sin, and it's a dangerous game to play. The second thing is that God gives warning through His

Holy Spirit. The third thing is that I can't keep leaning on my own understanding.

Today at church, I was in the New Members Perfecting Class. The teacher explained the different areas of ministries you could work in. One area was with the youth ministry. I felt like the youth ministry was an area I would like to work in because of everything I had been through as a teenager.

I feel like God has given me a gift to speak to others. The teacher agreed that she could see that gift in me and felt I would be a good role model. She also told me that she thinks I have a lot to give, more than I know. This made me realize that to tell others, I must first do what's right myself.

So now, dear God, I ask for your help. I pray that you lead and guide me in everything I am about to do. I pray that you give me strength so that the devil will have no place in my life. I pray I can go on and do great things.

In Jesus' name, I ask amen.

Storms are unpredictable! The forecast can call for a forty percent chance of rain, which may rain in one part of town, but not another. A tornado can head west, but one shift of the wind and suddenly it could be going north, south, or east. Life is pretty much the same way. Life can be sunny and bright one minute, and then a dark cloud appears out of nowhere without warning. Things were going pretty well with Jackson, but I was battling internally. After giving my life to God, I finally knew what it felt like to be in His presence. Now that I was spending so much time with Jackson, I wasn't spending as much time with God.

I found myself slipping away from God, who was the source of my strength and existence. Companionship was good, but I needed God more than anything to maintain a healthy balance. Jackson and I were getting closer and closer. I recall the day his parents visited our job at the Transco Towers on May 23rd, 1999. He gave his parents a tour of the observatory on the top floor, and I must say his mother was the sweetest person. They were celebrating their twenty-fourth wedding anniversary.

On May 30, 1999, Jackson and I went to the mall to buy them a gift. It was a pleasure to spend time with them and for Jackson to deem me worthy to meet them. Most men don't introduce a woman to their parents unless they are serious about pursuing a more profound relationship or marriage.

Spending time with Jackson and his family was very refreshing. But life taught me early on that it could be very unpredictable. You can never be prepared for the unexpected. On June 6, 1999, just days after meeting Jackson's mother, we received the news that she had passed. I was devastated for Jackson because I knew how it felt to lose a mother.

I was unsure how Jackson would take it, but he was strong, and I am happy that I was there to be his backbone. I am also delighted that I was the one to be the final chapter in his life in his mom's eyes, and because of that, I gave my all to ensure he knew I was there for him. His father told me how ecstatic Jackson's mom was to see her son happy before she passed and that she could rest in peace knowing he would be okay. Hearing those words was such a blessing to my soul.

I feel like I impacted his and his family's life. To think God predestined our paths to cross at the right time for all the right reasons. Just think I strongly disliked this man, who appeared to be cold and callous, but now we were in a relationship, and I was chosen to be by his side during such a difficult time. Jeremiah 29:11 tells us that God knows the plans He has for us. Even when we are lost and feeling out of sorts with life, God has the blueprint if we are willing to be patient and seek Him until His complete plan is revealed.

As I stood by Jackson, my prayer was that until we saw Jesus, God would keep His mercy, grace, and blessing upon us. As time went on and Jackson was working through the loss of his mother, we were growing closer and closer together. I felt safe with him, and the more time we spent together, the more I learned about his character and love language.

One Sunday, we were hanging around the house all day doing nothing when he said, "Let's go to the Water Wall!" I was somewhat shocked, being that is where he spent most of his time working. I wondered why he wanted to go there, of all places. I mean, it was a romantic place. I did not know what he had on his mind, but I said okay and went along with the plan.

The Water Wall was a popular place many people frequented to take wedding photos because of the vast wall of water falling, the large green lawn, and the over 50-floor building towering on the opposite side. When we arrived at the Water Wall, Jackson bought me a pink rose, and we went on a carriage ride. That is when he began digging in his pocket and pulled out this ring and pendant that belonged to his mother before she passed away.

Can you imagine the look on my face? I was absolutely shocked as I sat there with my heart beating a thousand miles per minute. I did not see this coming at all! Then he asked, "Tiwonna will you marry me?" and I remember asking, "Are you for real?" and he said, "Yes," and I said, "Yes." OMG! I could not believe I became an engaged woman after three months of dating on Sunday, August 1, 1999.

God says He will give you a future, hope, and an expected end, and He did just that. He told me to call and tell everybody, but the first person I told was my friend Brenda. Everybody was happy for us, including his dad, who had gotten engaged on the same day. I was so excited, but it was bittersweet because I wanted to call my mother and share this news with her, and I am sure Jackson was feeling the same.

We were about to embark on one of the most incredible adventures of our lives, and having our mothers walk us through the fears and shower us with love would have been fantastic, but God had other plans. We took comfort in knowing they would be with us in spirit.

Jackson and I encountered a few scattered storms and a couple of tornadoes, but God's favor and love caused us to triumph over the enemy. Meeting Jackson confirmed Psalm 37:23, "The Lord orders the steps of a righteous man." I didn't always feel like I was doing the right thing, but God continually showed me His mercy, which is sufficient in all things.

The enemy wanted me to get tossed up and destroyed in the whirlwind of life, but God protected me and caused me to land on my feet every time, and for that, I am eternally grateful.

Chapter Eight

"The Joy of My Salvation"

Journal Entry 8/18/1999

I would first like to thank the Lord God above for his grace, love, and kindness despite how I have behaved. It has been about three weeks since I haven't been to church, and I am starting to slack off more and more.

My relationship with Jackson is going very well. We just celebrated our three-month anniversary, but my job is now the problem. Me and my supervisor or not getting along. Good news, Jackson started a new job today. He got a promotion!

Today is the first day he worked on his own after his training. I am really happy for him and hope this move will bring us both bigger and better things. He is now the supervisor at St. Luke's Medical Tower in the medical center. I realized that what brought Jackson and I together was that we both were hard-working people who wanted something out of life. We both had a Christian background and shared the same beliefs about family.

Good news and bad news for me! My 1988 Honda Accord was stolen on August 6 and found a few days later. The vehicle was missing a few things, but I traded it for a 1997 Chevrolet Cavalier. The car is blue, so I nicknamed her True Blue.

I'm hoping I can cope better with my job when I start back attending church.

Living a life that is holy and acceptable to God can become challenging. No matter how much you attempt to walk the straight and narrow, it feels like there is always a bump in the road to knock you off course. Trying to maintain a relationship with God, myself, Jackson, and others were wearing me out because the most important relationship was suffering–my relationship with God. I was missing the joy of my salvation.

Don't get me wrong, I was happy and joyful to be in a relationship with Jackson, but God tells us not to put anything before Him, and I was well aware of this. My spirit man was being convicted daily because I wasn't on fire for God. I was slacking on attending church and doing the ministry work I knew I was called to do.

When I look back on my journal entry from August 18, 1999, it is very apparent that God was trying to get my attention. First, I started having issues with my job, and my car was stolen. Thank God Jackson was raised with a Christian foundation and wanted to do things right by getting married because the guilt was taking a toll on me.

I was constantly in my head, but God was continually trying to show me His love and how love covers a multitude of sins. All my prayers were being answered, and my Father was making ways out of no way for me. The first five months of my relationship with Jackson were terrific. He was so good to me that I always wanted to be surrounded by his love, kindness, and gentleness.

I felt so close to him that I could not do something or buy something for myself without thinking of him. I was always focused on myself, so this was a significant turnaround. The only thing lacking in the relationship was more of God by attending church, praying together, and giving God His time.

We were working hard and getting ready to plan a wedding. Time was limited, but not to the point where we couldn't make time for God. If He was not the center of our individual lives first and then the life we were forming, eventually, our lives would crumble.

Before Jackson and I became official, he told me he got married when he enlisted in the army. Jackson and his first wife were married less than a year before they separated. Jackson was in the army for less than two years before returning to Houston. He was initially enlisted in Georgia. After returning to Houston, he lost contact with his wife, but when I met him, he lived with his girlfriend.

These conditions were not favorable for us. Unresolved issues from the past were putting a damper on our future. Looking at this situation, everything within you would say it's not a good idea to be with a man that was still legally married and just left his girlfriend to move in with you. It was a chance I took and seeds I had sown that I would soon have to reap. At this point in my life, I would never advise or condone a woman or a man to be in a relationship with someone that is legally married.

Even after a divorce, I feel like counseling should take place. While developing a relationship with God through Jesus, I thought that I could still go against His will and reap His blessings. Yes, God is a gracious God, but we should in no way put our desires above His word. James 1:8 says, "A double-minded man is unstable in all his ways." During this phase of my life, I was very unstable, and I could feel myself pulling away from God and not towards God.

I am reminded of the story of David when he had a strong desire for Bathsheba, the wife of Uriah. David, a man after God's own heart, found himself lusting in his flesh for Bathsheba and made the worst mistake of his life. David summoned Bathsheba and committed adultery with her. The classic cliché says, "What's done in the dark will come to light." In David and Bathsheba's case, she became pregnant. David tried to cover up his indiscretion by calling Uriah back home to make him sleep with his wife, but he refused because he was adamant about not being intimate during the war.

Since plan A didn't work, David had to devise another strategy to cover his sin. He decided to put Uriah on the frontline and have him killed in battle. Unfortunately, this plan worked, and after Uriah's death, David took Bathsheba as his wife, but God neither slumbers nor sleeps. David may have pulled the wool over man's eyes, but God's eyes were upon him.

Bathsheba carried the baby, but the baby was struck with sickness. David was prostrate before the Lord, begging and pleading for mercy and forgiveness, asking God not to take his child, but after three days of fasting and praying, the baby passed. In Psalm 51, you will find David praying and asking God to restore unto him the joy of his salvation. This didn't mean that David was no longer saved. It simply meant he stepped out of the will of God, fell weak in his flesh, and needed his spirit to be restored.

Like David, I knew what I wanted and was convinced that Jackson was my husband, but putting him before God would prove to be the biggest mistake of my life. I needed God to cleanse my heart and renew the right spirit within me. My heart was open to Jackson, but it belonged to God first and foremost. I especially needed God to fix the situation with Jackson's previous marriage.

He hired a lawyer to find his ex-wife, and it seemed like the lawyer was just taking our money. One day out of the clear blue sky, his ex-wife called his dad's house, and his dad took down all her information because he knew what we were trying to do. After calling her, she said she had moved on and was with someone else and wanted the divorce; the rest was history. In 2000 Jackson's divorce was final, and it seemed like it took a miracle from God.

I was so excited to see God move in this situation. I felt so far from Him, but He was working behind the scenes all along. While condemning myself, God was teaching me the power of His unfailing love. I learned that God is faithful and gives good things to His children who love Him. Even though David lost the child conceived in adultery, God blessed him and Bathsheba with another son we know as the wisest man to ever live– King Solomon.

God will take what the enemy meant for evil and allow it to work for your good and to bring glory to Him as a sovereign God. I was so focused on the tangible things that I failed to understand that God blesses us according to the condition of our hearts. Jackson and I were not perfect, but we loved God, worked hard, and allowed Him to order our steps and direct our paths.

Chapter Nine

"It Wasn't For Nothing"

"We know that all things work together for the good of those who love God, who are called according to his purpose." Romans 8:28

Bishop T. D. Jakes preached a sermon in 2012 entitled, "Nothing You Have Been Through Will Be Wasted." This would mean that all the trials, traumas, heartaches, pains, losses, failures, and disappointments are God-ordained. So many times in life, we tend to see the pain of life as punishment and not purpose. James told us to think it not strange when different trials and temptations happen in our lives because they come to test and teach us how to depend on God.

After losing my mother, I encountered many trials and traumas that forced me to depend on God because man showed me their true colors. I was bitter but soon realized I was right where God wanted and needed me to be. I never met my biological father, but God proved to be a Father who would provide good things and unconditional love for me as His daughter.

My assignment in writing this book is two-fold. One was to share my testimony of grace and mercy with the world, and two was to shine the light on the glorious wonders of God our Father. Despite all I have encountered, God has never left or forsaken me. Even in my darkest moments, operating from a broken place and making ungodly, unwise choices, He still showed me mercy and provided my every need.

No one wants to suffer hardship, and even though our stories may differ, the pain mostly feels the same. From the beginning, man has been fighting an internal battle with the flesh warring against the spirit. As you can see from the beginning of my life journey, my foundation was not solid. I was like the man in the bible whose house was built on sand, and the house fell when the storms came.

But the adversities I faced were meant to tear down the unstable foundation so that God could rebuild my life on the cornerstone of Jesus Christ. I was so happy when I gave my life to Christ because I felt the change, and I knew God loved me and saved me for His purpose. That is why I struggled so much when I failed to attend church or give God His time because I would never have made it without Him.

I could have easily followed my mother's destructive path because children are like sponges. They tend to do or become what was modeled in front of them. Thankfully I picked up my mother's skills to do hair because it proved to be a blessing when needed. I am forever grateful that God covered and protected me from her self-destructive patterns.

Deuteronomy 1:31 says, *"And you saw how the Lord your God cared for you all along the way as you traveled through the wilderness, just as a father cares for his child. Now he has brought you to this place."*

I love the place that God has brought me to in my life. There is still much to do and learn, but today I understand I was created for greatness, and sometimes greatness is birth out of pain. God uses every part of our lives as a testimony of who He is and an encouragement of hope and faith to others. He is a resourceful God and never allows anything to be wasted. Need proof? Even after Satan was cast out of heaven, God still uses Him to accomplish His will on earth. Satan can't do anything without permission or instruction from God, his creator.

God also stores up our tears. Psalm 56:8 says, "You keep track of all my sorrows. You have collected all my tears in your bottle. You have recorded each one in your book." I cried many days and nights, wondering when my situation would change, crying for my mother, and wishing to know my father. Crying for a stable home and not to be rejected. I was crying to be treated like a human being and not a benefit for those who were left to care for me in my mother's absence. But God!

He stored up those tears, and at the appointed time, He took the tears He collected and poured them out over my life to water my land that would eventually produce a plentiful harvest. When God blesses, He makes you rich, and no sorrow is added. Jackson was an unexpected blessing that added value to life. He came from a stable household, and mine was unbalanced, so he offered the balance I needed and longed for my entire life.

God made my crooked ways straight, and I watched as the mountains in my life began to crumble and create a new path for me to walk on. I may have been rejected in my life, but I know it wasn't for nothing. God used it all to make me a better woman, girlfriend, employee, church member, sister, and so much more. He used my adversities to build character and prepare me for a fruitful future, but I had to allow Him to put the puzzle pieces of my life together without getting in the way. I had to surrender my will to His will and trust His blueprint for my life.

So many different life pieces had to be connected to reach an expected end. Our lives are constructed much like a puzzle because we only know in part, but God knows all things. He knows what our lives are supposed to look like, but we often struggle because we don't know, so we grab at this person, job, church, or coping mechanism, hoping that something works.

We attempt to take shortcuts in life that keep us going around the mountain like the children of Israel, year after year. Putting a puzzle together takes patience, time, dedication, and commitment, and so does life. God is a lamp unto our feet and a light unto our path, which means we will never be able to live a prosperous life without Him directing us. When I decided to stop leaning on my own understanding and started acknowledging Him in all His ways, doors opened for me, and my dreams became a reality.

Journal Entry 7/29/2000

Today July 29, 2000, would have been my mother Gloria's 44th birthday, and it is also the day I am getting married.

The day had finally come when I would walk down the aisle to become Mrs. Jackson Moore. I could not believe that I was going to be Jackson's wife and to think, at some point, the mother of his children. Getting married was a dream come true. Something I envisioned for my life but had no idea when it would manifest. A prayer answered by the Lord who knew the person and the time.

I chose to get married on July 29, 2000, in honor of my mother, who would have celebrated her 44th birthday. I longed to see her face, her smile, and to hear her voice. I could envision her doing my hair and helping me with the wedding jitters and those Bridezilla moments. She would have been so proud to see her baby girl get married, but God knows best.

My beautiful mother was resting in the presence of the Lord. I accepted that she would be with me in spirit, and getting married on her birthday allowed me to honor her and keep her memory alive. In the future, July 29th would be a Happy Heavenly Birthday to my mom and Happy Anniversary for Jackson and I.

Now if the enemy tested me during the foundational years of my life, you could rest assured that I was tested even more after giving my life to Christ and tying the knot to become one with Jackson. You know the enemy hates covenant and will do anything to destroy the family origin created by God in the Garden.

It wasn't for nothing, but the "it" didn't stop, and the fiery darts kept coming and almost took me out!

Chapter Ten

"Why Me, Lord?"

After examining myself and conviction by the Holy Spirit, I have come to recognize who I am and the things that are most important to me or not always important to God. Sometimes we can get so mixed up in the things we want to do and things we want to have that there is no room for God. I have been asking God to reveal the things He wants for me and reveal my wrongdoing, but what good is it when I reject what he has shown me?

One day I told the Lord I would follow Him and never turn back, but sometimes we get afraid of where we are being taken and turn back for the earlier route. But I realize that when we give ourselves to Christ, we've been bought with the blood of Jesus. We must take up our cross and walk down that uncertain road in faith and love. When we pick up that cross, we can't carry ourselves and the cross, so we must leave ourselves and take up the cross so that Christ's light will shine through us because self has too much darkness, and darkness and light can't have fellowship.

So, in other words, I must repent, for I have sinned, not only against myself but against my brothers and sisters to whom I should be an example. I have grieved the Holy Spirit by not listening to His instructions. I have also sinned by allowing the spirit of slumber to enter my life by wasting time. Repentance is critical in the life of a Christian, and I thank God for His grace. David said God knew his frame, meaning God knew him according to his strengths and weaknesses.

He knew that no matter what he did, as long as he sought the face of God, everything would be alright. It took me some time to grasp this concept because man holds you accountable for everything and constantly reminds you of your indiscretions. God says He will forgive our sins and remember them no more. After setting my spiritual life in order, it was time to make some moves naturally.

I decided to go back to school to get my cosmetology license. I worked in security for four years and was becoming uncomfortable. It started to feel like the walls were closing in on me. My job was very easy. I sat in the lobby of a fifty-five-story building looking at cameras. I knew that hair was my purpose, but I got stuck. I worked nights, Thursday through Sunday, and went to school Monday through Thursday in the mornings. I only had four months left, so it was worth the sacrifice.

I thank God for Jackson because I don't think I would have been able to finish without him. Before we got together, I worked a lot of overtime for extra money, but two incomes helped us both. I finally felt like I was doing what I was meant to do. I felt like my life had a purpose, and more than anything, I was honoring my mother's legacy.

After getting my cosmetology license, it was still hard for me to step out on faith and apply for a job in my career. I remember working security in the Galleria Mall and passing by Visible Changes, thinking, "One day, I'm going to work here." I would walk the long way around just to pass by the salon to smell the products and see the lights.

I got the courage one day and applied for the job at Visible Changes, but they didn't have an opening in the Galleria. They had an opening at another salon closer to my house, so I took the job there. I must admit I had to get used to being woke when my body was used to sleeping and standing on my feet all day instead of sitting down all night.

I started losing a lot of weight which was good for me, but now it appeared that Jackson and I hardly had time for each other. He took a new position as a supervisor, and I was still trying to adjust to my new work schedule. I worked weekends when he was off, and I worked the evening shift when he was getting off work. After seven months, I realized that most of the people I worked with lived at work to get ahead.

They were very proud of their sacrifices to climb the ladder of success, which only gave them around fifty percent of the money they earned. But I wanted to spend time with my family, so I applied for a job at a slower pace salon where I worked six hours a day on average. I loved this job. It was a family salon where the whole family would come and get haircuts and prom updos, and little old ladies would come early in the day to get their perms.

Not long after starting this job, I found out I was pregnant. It seemed like everything was coming into place. Jackson and I had just moved into a bigger place where there would be a room for the baby. I was so excited about being a mother.

The rush of emotions was overwhelming because we were so happy. I was determined that my child would never have to experience the things I did as a child. Thankfully we were already in a better place because I was married to the father and in church. This baby would be covered in prayer from the womb until it enters the earth and every day after. Again, this was a bittersweet moment because I could not share the news with my mom, nor would she be here to walk me through and support me in the delivery room.

The pregnancy went great, but Jackson seemed to be off in some areas. I figured I may have been overreacting and just hormonal from the pregnancy. I tried not to put too much thought into it because the mind can be tricky and deceptive.

Journal Entry 10/8/2003

I went to the doctor for my forty-week check-up. At my appointment, I was told I was one centimeter dilated and should go to the hospital. TeYonna was due October 10, 2003, but it looks like she is coming a day earlier. At 10:30 am, I was induced. My labor started at 7:00 pm. At 2:21 am Te'Yonna Moore was born. My feelings overwhelmed me. I cried with excitement that this was my daughter. I was sad because my mother couldn't be here to share this moment with me.

After TeYonna's birth, everything seemed to be perfect. My husband took off work to be home with us while I recovered. We took turns waking up at night to care for the baby. It was a transition for both of us because it had been just us, and now we had a whole human to clothe, bathe, feed, and take with us everywhere we went.

Eventually, I returned to church after taking the job at the new salon. I would get off early on Wednesday to attend bible study. My husband's cousin kept our daughter while I went to work, and depending on our schedule, we would pick her up from the babysitter. Life couldn't be better from where I was looking. We had the perfect little family, and I didn't think anything could happen to ruin what we were building.

Remember when I said things with Jackson were off and chalked it up to pregnancy hormones? Well, it just so happens my hormones may have been out of control, but I wasn't wrong about the change in his demeanor. After three years and five months, Jackson walked out on our two-and-a-half-month-old daughter and me on December 29, 2003. I mean, what a way to start the new year!

There are no words to express the hurt, pain, disappointment, rejection, and betrayal I felt at that moment. I was numb mentally, emotionally, and spiritually. Disbelief turned to hurt, and hurt turned to anger. One day I sat listening and reflecting on Anita Baker's song, "No Fairy Tales." The words go something like this,

"I can remember stories, those things my mother said.
She told me fairy tales before I went to bed.
She spoke of happy endings, then tucked me in

real tight. She turned my night light on and kissed my face good night.
My mind was filled with visions of a perfect paradise.
She told me everything; she said he'd be so nice.
He'd ride up on his horse and take me away one night.
I'd be so happy with him; we'd ride clean out of sight.
She never said that we would curse, cry and scream and lie.
She never said that maybe, someday, he'd say goodbye.
The story ends, as stories do
Reality steps into view
No longer living life in paradise, of fairy tales."

So many times, we try to build realities on Fairy Tales! Relationships are not supposed to be fifty-fifty because relationship math is unlike numerical mathematics. Each person is responsible for entering the relationship as a whole person.

Whole means perfection according to God's standards, not men. The truth of the matter is brokenness brought us together. Two broken people who thought we would somehow make each other whole. There was no cursing, crying, and screaming, but there were strongholds of the soul. Silence is not always golden. There was this quietness in the eye of the storm, but now the storm was about to pass over us.

At the time, I wasn't praying as I should have. But I thank God I was warned before the storm came and began to get in his will. The Holy Spirit revealed some details because He will not leave you ignorant of satans devices.

The Bible tells us to pray without ceasing because we never know when the enemy will strike. We need to have our armor on at all times to ensure that the blood covers us and the angels of heaven watch over us. I tried desperately not to blame myself for his choices, but I couldn't help but wonder where I had gone wrong. Was it when I was working too many hours? Was it because I wasn't praying enough?

I was raised without a father and lost my mother at an early age, and I was not about to let this curse interfere with my daughter's future. She needed her father in her life, so I was prepared to fight, but I was not going to fight alone. I had the Holy Trinity on my side–God, Jesus, and the Holy Spirit and I was ready to partner up to save my husband from the enemy's camp.

Journal Entry 1/7/2004

I have made up my mind to let the past be the past. All I can do is pray that his eyes become open and that my hurt for what he has done to this family will go. I realize I have to have some contact with him because of our daughter.

But there is no denying the bitterness and hurt I want him to feel just as I feel. Today I vow to take care of my daughter, work hard, so we suffer no financial lack, go to church, and pray so that I can be right with God the Father. I believe that no matter the situation, God our Father will never forsake us.

The hardest thing to do in the midst of hurt, bitterness, and loss of a relationship is to look in the mirror and see the part we play. Emotional pain can sometimes block our view of what landed us in the situation, and the first response is to hold on tighter to the stronghold. A stronghold is a place of security or survival. Strongholds can be good and bad. If we allow God to be our stronghold in times of trouble, we can find that security in Him. But so many times, we find security in the things of this world.

We find security in the lust of the flesh, the lust of the eyes and the pride of life. My response to my husband leaving was that I would work harder so that my daughter and I wouldn't suffer any lack and that I would go to church and pray to be right with the Father. I thought my relationship with the church meant I had a relationship with God. I thought having a marriage certificate would make me a wife and him a husband, but this was so far from the truth.

Chapter Eleven

"What Is Love?"

Journal Entry 12/17/2004

"What Is Love?" You once asked me what is love.

I answered, "Love is God, and God is love. That's very true, but that wasn't the answer you were looking for.

Love is patient, kind, and unfailing - Long Suffering! Love doesn't walk out when times get hard. Love doesn't do what it feels like doing, but it does what it should, the right thing. Love is not selfish. It does not think about how it feels and leaves the other hanging.

Love remembers not only the bad but the good. Love sticks together and doesn't give up. Love is unfailing. Love is not a feeling.

Love is a commitment to an almighty God. Love never fails.

It's sad to say, but I knew very little about love at twenty-seven years old. But I was about to learn all about being patient and kind, and I dare not talk about long-suffering. The saying that there are two sides to every story is true. We often tell the story from our side and not God's side.

After receiving divorce papers one day at work, I wondered how a beautiful sunny day could be so dark and painful. The gentleman who served the papers was nice enough to call me before he arrived. He said he would call when he was outside to spare me the embarrassment of signing the divorce papers in front of my co-workers at the receptionist's desk. The pain of going through a divorce is so dreadful I remember losing track of time, but that day was a pivotal point in my life.

I waited to get home to open the divorce papers because I knew I would be emotional but reading them somehow empowered me. I remember thinking to myself, I have thirty-one days to answer back to this divorce decree, but I have twenty-one days to fast. I wasn't big on fasting, but I had already lost about twenty pounds due to stress, so I didn't have much of an appetite anyways.

I did a three-day fast here and there, but twenty-one days with one week of only liquids would push me to the limit. I felt like I had everything to lose, so I had to do it. I remember the Holy

Spirit took me to Ephesians 6:10-18 (KJV): *For we wrestle not against flesh and blood, but against principalities, against powers, against the rulers of the darkness of this world, against spiritual wickedness in high places. Wherefore take unto you the whole armor of God, that ye may be able to withstand in the evil day, and having done all, to stand. Stand therefore, having your loins girt about with truth, and having on the breastplate of righteousness; and your feet shod with the preparation of the gospel of peace; above all, taking the shield of faith, wherewith ye shall be able to quench all the fiery darts of the wicked. And take the helmet of salvation, and the sword of the Spirit, which is the word of God: praying always with all prayer and supplication in the Spirit and watching thereunto with all perseverance and supplication for all saints. Finally, my brethren, be strong in the Lord, and in the power of his might. Put on the whole armor of God, that ye may be able to stand against the wiles of the devil. '*

The Holy Spirit showed me that I had been fighting with carnal and not spiritual weapons. It's like showing up for a gunfight empty-handed. Satan has no power over our lives when we submit to Christ and receive the victory only found in Him. That day I made sure I had the armor on, which was on tightly. I began to do things on purpose and with a purpose. The first thing I did was start reading my bible regularly.

I read the Bible because our only weapon is His word. There was no Google or YouTube, so I had to go to the back of the bible and do a word search. I looked up marriage and divorce, and what I found gave me a blueprint.

In the Old Testament, I found that Moses' law allowed the man (not the woman) to write a divorce letter to the woman, and he would be free. Jesus came along and said that if the man divorced his wife for any other reason other than sexual immorality, this would be adultery. Paul said two things that gave me hope. The first was that if I were living a Godly life, I would win my husband over, but if he wanted to leave, then let him leave.

As I spent time with the Lord, I began to realize that, at times, God will allow situations that only He can get you out of to show that He is God by Himself. I often thought about where I would be if I didn't go through the things I encountered.

Trials strengthened and helped me to focus on God. At one point, I acted as if Jackson was my savior. I often wondered what I would be without him and realized I'd be right where I started, depending on my Heavenly Father. Sometimes we bypass God and look to man because we want something we can see, touch, and smell. But I have realized that we must not depend on our five senses.

So, we don't look at the troubles we can see now; rather, we fix our gaze on things that cannot be seen. For the things we see now will soon be gone, but the things we cannot see will last forever. 2 Corinthians 4:18 (NLT)

I believed if I could receive revelation and wisdom from this scripture and live according to it, life as I know it would be lived in a different light. I thank God for what happened to me, and God was so awesome that amid destruction (as I knew it), God was blessing me.

I thank God for the sunshine in my life, my daughter. Whenever I opened my eyes, I didn't have time to think about what was happening around me. When I saw those big bright eyes and that full smile, it lit my heart up. I couldn't help but smile with her and thank God, He gave her to me. The one thing I asked of the Lord is that He would be to her what He was to me—a very present help in times of trouble.

I pray to be a godly example and that my lifestyle would lead her to Christ. I thank God for Jackson's cousin Shelia who moved in with me and helped me with Te'Yonna. I prayed to help her as much as she was helping me. I asked the Lord to allow me to lead and show others what He had shown me. I prayed that He would give me the strength to run the race and continue to show me favor and show Himself strong on my behalf.

And the LORD God called unto Adam, and said unto him, Where art thou? And he said, I heard thy voice in the garden, and I was afraid because I was naked; and I hid myself. Genesis 3:9-10 (KJV)

Women tend to go into relationships with unrealistic expectations. We fall in love with a made-up version of what we want. In the early stages of dating, we show that person the version of who we want them to see. But then there comes a time when the real person shows up, and we wonder what happened. We often want them to give us what they can't give. It's just not in them. It's like wanting eight ounces of water in a four-ounce bottle.

Simply put, we fall in love with a make-believe person. You may ask how does this happen? For one, we ignore the signs and don't have discernment. *So, the Lord God asked the woman, "What have you done?" And the woman said, "The serpent deceived me, and I ate." Genesis 3:13 (KJV)* It's almost like we see history repeating itself.

The woman is deceived, but it's not always Satan deceiving because *self-deception* is the worst form of deception. Let me pose another point, *right person, wrong time.*

After receiving the divorce papers, I remember looking through the phone book for a lawyer. There were so many divorce attorneys that I didn't know where to start, so I just started dialing. The first few said the same about paying a pricey retainer fee that I couldn't afford. I stopped calling and prayed. I returned to the phone book and saw a name that stood out. I dialed the number, and this compassionate female lawyer answered the phone.

She stated that she could hear the hurt in my voice and extended the offer for me to visit her office. She agreed to look over the divorce decree at no charge and would let me know what she could do. After going to her office that same week, she told me it wouldn't be a lengthy process because we didn't have any assets together. She was kind enough to call my husband and ask him a few questions about the paperwork.

She made a statement that I'll never forget. She said, "It seems like you all are meant to be together, but your timing is off." I learned, "The right person at the wrong time equals the wrong person." Not only was the timing off for him but for me also. I needed to grow up. I needed to heal and find out who I was in Christ. I was about to take off the fig leaves of rejection, abandonment, and pride to receive the glory I was meant to be covered with.

Chapter Twelve

"Midnight Burden"

The midnight hour is the dawning of a brand-new day. I was in a dark place, longing for God to show up and bring peace to every area of my life, especially my marriage. When I think about midnight, I am reminded of Paul and Silas, who were in jail in chains, but when midnight came, they started praising God, and the chains fell off. When the chains fell off, the angel of the Lord opened the prison gate and led them out. Have you ever been in a situation where you felt trapped and did not know what to do?

Going through a divorce was never part of the plan. I didn't have many examples other than my godparents of a successful marriage because my mother never married. I found myself journaling the following prayer:

Lord, I need strength. The gap that I must stand in is wide. The burden is too heavy. But I hear you calling me for a greater work. I write this with tears and much sorrow. Sorrow for the world that I am living in, where the fathers should be the priest and protectors in the home.

It saddens my heart. I am so hurt that this is the world I am to raise my daughter in—a world where the hearts of men have forsaken God and thereby abandoned the post. I want to protect my daughter so badly, but it's like sending her into this world as a sheep among wolves.

Faith has shown me that the prayers of the righteous prevaileth much. Father, help me keep your commandments. I know you will help me carry this burden and prepare me for war.

Put on all of God's armor so that you will be able to stand firm against all strategies of the devil. For we are not fighting against flesh-and-blood enemies, but against evil rulers and authorities of the unseen world, against mighty powers in this dark world, and against evil spirits in the heavenly places. Ephesians 6:11-12 (NLT)

I researched every scripture I could find on marriage. At first, it wasn't very encouraging until I found 1 Corinthians 7:14-16 (NLT), which says, *"For the believing wife brings holiness to her marriage, and the believing husband*

110

brings holiness to his marriage. Otherwise, your children would not be holy, but now they are holy. (But if the husband or wife who isn't a believer insists on leaving, let them go. In such cases, the believing husband or wife is no longer bound to the other, for God has called you to live in peace.) Don't you wives realize that your husbands might be saved because of you? And don't you husbands realize that your wives might be saved because of you?"

I found the spiritual weapon I needed to fight for my marriage. I realized the blame wasn't on my husband alone, but I was also a part of the problem. Years of rejection caused me to become prideful.

I didn't give my husband the respect he needed as a man. I would punish him with silent treatment when he disagreed with what I said until he saw things my way. We were both young and immature kids when we got married. I also felt like I reaped what I had sown, entering a relationship with him before his divorce was finalized. I disobeyed God's command, and this became idolatry.

I put my selfish wants above God's word and masked this idolatry with wedding vows. But the idolatry was still there. I put my husband before God. When he didn't go to church, I didn't go. I would always say, "I would have bet my life that he wouldn't have done me like this, and I would've been a dead woman," until one day,

God said, "The life you have isn't yours to give." I repented, drew closer to God, and enjoyed time in His word and praying. I stopped praying for Jackson to return to me and for him to come to God.

Journal Entry 6/14/2004

Thinking back to when I first received this diary, I never thought I would be writing part of my life story in it. I received this diary while working at the church day camp. I believe it was my last summer. Now I'm twenty-seven years old, working two jobs, raising my eight-month-old daughter, going through a divorce, and have no clue what tomorrow will bring.

As I grew stronger in the Lord, I still had my days. I would feel alone, wondering how I got here—days of disbelief. Yet there was this knowing inside me that God had a plan for life, and somehow this would work out for my good. My daughter would wake up at 6 am, and after feeding her, I would take that time to pray.

I remember the Lord telling me to stop talking to Him. He said He couldn't hear His voice because of mine. So many times, we as women feel that we are justified because we speak the truth, but if we aren't using wisdom as it pertains to our approach, it'll never be received. Many times, the correction shouldn't come from us. I was trying to be the Father, Son, and the Holy Spirit. My position as his wife was to cover him in prayer and allow the Holy Spirit to work on his heart.

When I allowed God to take the wheel and I jumped in the passenger seat, life started to shift in my direction. Let me say that PRAYER works!!!!!!!!!!!!!!!!! Jackson and I reconciled on June 20th. I didn't think he would return so soon, so I started moving on but never gave up hope. I mean, what is hope anyway? But, no matter, I never stop hoping against hope.

I hoped I could trust him again. I hoped he did not return because of a last alternative. I told Jackson if he didn't love me that, maybe we should call it quits (in so many words). He said he returned because he loved me and knew we should be together, but his actions showed me something different. Now I needed to know what to do because only God knows the heart. But I needed God to tell me if I should guard mine.

Should I put a shield over my heart and only let him close but not let him in? I prayed for the day he would come to God and me, but now that he was back, I didn't know how to move forward. The night we got back together was nothing short of a miracle. God told me to stop bugging him so he could hear from Him. So, I did! No more texting scriptures about how he was going against God's word, no more being vindictive, and no more fighting in the flesh.

I was up late one night reading my bible, which was odd because I would wake up at six in the morning after fixing Te'Yonna's bottle and stay up praying after she went back to sleep. The Lord said, "Call your husband" I didn't think it was God because He told me to leave him alone. But I felt like God was pressing me to call him, so I did. It was awkward because I didn't know why I was calling him, so I just asked him how he was doing. And he said, "Not so good." Then I said, "Why, what's wrong?" He replied, "I made the biggest mistake of my life when I left my family." I was speechless. I was only a few days off my twenty-one-day fast, and I couldn't believe what God had done in his heart that fast.

I couldn't believe what he had done in my heart either. He told me that life wasn't worth living because he had messed up his family. I feared he would hurt himself, so I went to his apartment. I prayed with him, but I told him he could come to my apartment because of how he sounded. Thankfully he came with me.

I learned so much through this experience, and as crazy as it might sound, I wouldn't change what happened. I learned so much about myself, God's word, spiritual warfare, my own weaknesses, and how to be a wife. Only what's built on the rock will stand. I remember tearing those divorce papers into pieces.

Jackson never went back to that apartment to live. He moved in with me, and we worked on rebuilding our marriage which wasn't too hard because I kept God first and allowed him to lead, guide, and direct. When we first got married, we prayed together, and as he prayed in the Holy Spirit, I saw a vision of my husband singing in the church choir. I never told my husband about the vision, but it kept me fighting for our marriage.

Shortly after we had gotten back together and we both became more faithful with going to church, my husband joined the choir and led his first song. It was just as I saw it in the vision God gave me. I cried like a baby that Sunday at church.

I have observed something else under the sun. The fastest runner doesn't always win the race, and the strongest warrior doesn't always win the battle. The wise sometimes go hungry, and the skillful are not necessarily wealthy. And those who are educated don't always lead successful lives. It is all decided by chance, by being in the right place at the right time. People can never predict when hard times might come. Like fish in a net or birds in a trap, people are caught by sudden tragedy. Ecclesiastes 9:11-12 (NLT)

Ecclesiastes 9:11-12 should be our 911 scriptures because there is no way to plan or control what happens during the uncertainty of our lives.

When things were uncertain in my life, it would have been easy to lean to my own understanding, but I went to God. I could have allowed pride and rebellion to destroy me and my family, but I chose to rely on the power of the Holy Spirit.

During the midnight hour, I chose to stand on the word of God, and in His timing, He broke the chains of divorce and restored my marriage. The best thing we can do as we walk down this path called life is to know the One that knows all and controls all. If you don't know Jesus Christ as your Lord and Savior, I pray you will accept Him into your life. Please get to know Him through the power of His word and allow His Holy Spirit to guide and direct your path.

Now let me tell the truth and nothing but the truth! God restored my marriage and bought our family back together, but that didn't mean the enemy wouldn't attempt to come in other ways. He knew I had the war strategy down pact regarding my family, so quite naturally, he had to go back to the drawing board and come again.

Can you imagine the blessings, challenges, spiritual battles, and divine interventions that awaited this young family as they built on the foundation of their faith? I guess you will have to find out in the next book because–

Life's Chronicles continues...

Author Bio

Tiwonna R. Moore

Tiwonna is passionate about women and has worked in ministry with young girls ages 11 to 21. She also served in a women's ministry at a local church for several years and now serves at her local church as a minister and assistant to her husband.

Tiwonna also has a prophetic anointing on her life that allows her to speak to the pre-destined purpose of those she ministers to. She is a licensed cosmetologist and CEO of My Glory Product Line.

Tiwonna loves to write and has done so since middle school. "The Chronicles of Life: It Wasn't for Nothing" is the first book in a series.

Tiwonna serves the intercessory prayer ministry at her local church and serves on the Palace of Praise prayer line. She has been an intercessor for over ten years in various ministries. She hosts and facilitates the "Iron Sharpening Iron Women's Conference Line."

Tiwonna and her husband have an Evangelistic Deliverance Ministry and serve as Assistant Pastors at the Palace of Praise Cleveland Church in Cleveland, Texas.

Tiwonna resides in Houston, Texas, with her husband, Pastor Jackson C. Moore, and two children Te'Yonna Moore and Jackson Tyler Moore.

Contact Information

Website(s): www.mygloryproductline.com
www.tiwonnarmoore.com
Facebook: @TiwonnaMoore
Instagram: @mooretiwonna

Made in the USA
Columbia, SC
07 October 2023

24088792R00065